Dear dear Thea,
Happy Happy Birthday to You!!!
How wonderful that you are 3
today! This is a book Nathan and
Sage read together with me,
when they were wee ones.
Happy Day!
Love you lots,
Sophie,
Sage
Nathan
xox

SMUDGE

SMUDGE

Story and Pictures by

CLARE TURLAY NEWBERRY

To Janet Rae

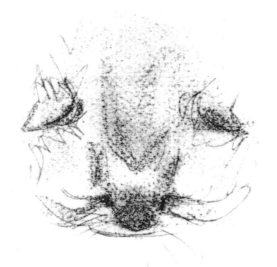

MUFF was delighted with her
new kittens. She purred and purred.

Buster, the big red father cat, was not half so pleased. He had never seen such tiny kittens before and they were not at all what he had expected. In his opinion they looked rather like mice, though he did not say so out loud.

There were three of them, two boys and a girl. The red one, who took after his father, was called Junior. The black one was called Smudge.

And the little black, white, and red girl kitten was named Betty Jo, after an aunt on her mother's side of the family.

At first the kittens did nothing
but eat and sleep. They did
not even open their eyes.

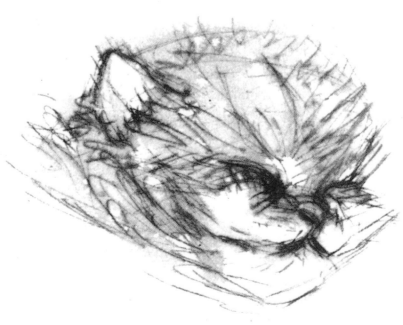

But every day they grew a little fatter
and a little fluffier. And every day they
looked more like kittens.

When Buster got used to his children he became quite fond of them. He liked to help with their bath, and he often stayed in the box with them while Muff got out to stretch her legs.

When the kittens were ten days old their eyes opened.

Soon after that they learned to walk, waddling about

unsteadily on their short legs, with their tails sticking

up like little pine trees.

Presently they began to wonder about the world outside their box and to stand on tiptoe to look over the edge.

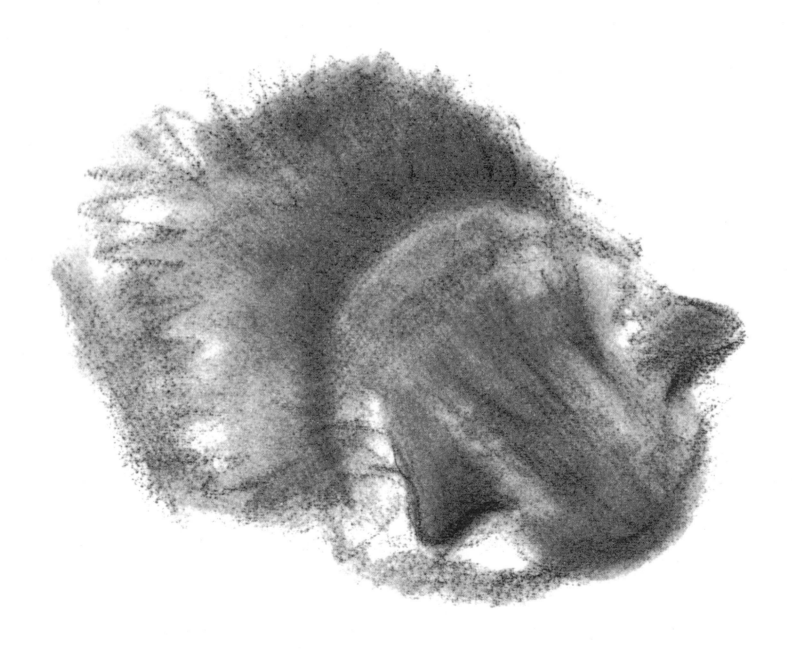

One day Muff and Buster decided that the children were old enough to be left alone for awhile, and they went out in the garden to chase grasshoppers. No one realized that the kittens had grown large enough to climb out of their box. But they had!

Smudge, who was the bravest, was the first over the side. Junior quickly followed. And then Betty Jo.

There they were, in a big room, full of ominous-looking furniture. But the kittens wisely took no chances.

They crept very quietly all over the place, sniffing

everything to see if it were dangerous.

However, when nothing growled, or barked, or

pounced at them they forgot to be afraid and

began to play.

Little Betty Jo crawled under a rug and hid. She was pretending to be a wild kitten in the woods, and the rug was her cave.

Junior made believe the window curtain was an enemy and attacked it savagely with all his teeth and claws.

It was a fierce battle, but Junior won, without a doubt.
For when the fight was over the window curtain was
full of holes, and Junior didn't have a scratch!

Then Smudge, who was a very brave kitten, climbed up the side of the sofa and jumped onto the table. There he found a marvelous plaything—a lamp with a fine silk shade that you could really get your claws into. And by standing on tiptoe and reaching, he did get his claws into it. He tugged and tugged, while the lamp rocked on its base. He tugged some more, and suddenly the whole thing toppled over. And with Smudge still clinging to it—for he didn't have time to unhook his claws—they crashed to the floor.

"Me-OW!" shrieked Smudge. Tearing loose his claws he scrambled under the sofa, followed by Junior and Betty Jo, who were almost as frightened as he was.

With their eyes round and their fur standing on end they watched the fallen lamp to see what it would do next. But the lamp did not move. It just lay there on the floor, all broken to pieces.

"*Prr-t! Prr-t! Prr-t!*" called Muff anxiously when she heard Smudge cry, and she rushed back into the house. Buster followed at a more leisurely pace. He was fond of the children but he did not worry over them as Muff did.

"*Mew! Mew! Mew!*" cried the kittens, running out from under the sofa to meet their mother. They knew the lamp could not hurt them if she were there. Muff sniffed them all over very carefully and was greatly relieved to find that they still had all their paws and tails and whiskers.

Just the same she did not like to have them running about in the room, where anything might happen, and she told them so, over and over, in cat language. Then she seized Smudge by the scruff of his neck and dragged him back to the box and plopped him in. She returned for Junior, and finally for Betty Jo. When they were all three safe in the box again she leapt in with them and washed them with her rough pink tongue.

That night the kittens were very hungry after all their adventures. And after supper they were very tired. When bedtime came do you suppose they begged Muff to tell them another story? Or teased Buster to let them stay up five minutes longer? Of course not.

They just snuggled up close to their warm furry

mother, and purred themselves to sleep.